Sybil Woolmore, the youngest of six siblings, was born in Auckland and raised on a remote sheep and cattle farm on the west coast of the North Island of New Zealand. She has always been a very independent person having been sent off to boarding school at aged 13 and then going flatting straight from school. She had no children but inherited two wonderful step children.

She enjoyed art for many years, selling several paintings and it wasn't until they retired and moved to Paeroa from Auckland seven years ago that she started writing and joined a newly formed writing group. She is inspired by life and people around her.

I would like to dedicate this book, firstly to my mum and dad, who always taught me that I could achieve anything I wanted if I was prepared to put in the work and boldly step out and not be afraid of failing, but learning from it.

And of course, my amazing husband, Ken, who has put up with me for 48 years, who dutifully listens to my writings (well sometimes anyway) and tries not to roll his eyes too much when another one comes to light.

Sybil Woolmore

The Way I See It

AUSTIN MACAULEY PUBLISHERS™

LONDON • CAMBRIDGE • NEW YORK • SHARJAH

A CIP catalogue record for this title is available from the British Library.

ISBN 9781035843787 (Paperback)
ISBN 9781035843794 (ePub e-book)

www.austinmacauley.co.uk

First Published 2024
Austin Macauley Publishers Ltd®
1 Canada Square
Canary Wharf
London
E14 5AA

I would like to acknowledge my very special friend, Kathy Thickpenny, who has always been so excited when I'd send through a new poem and has always been extremely encouraging. She has been a treasured friend since 1967 when I started my first job.

And Glenys Lewis, who set up the writers' group in Paeroa nearly seven years ago and encouraged me to go along. She has been the inspiration for many of the poems, giving the writers a fortnightly challenge. I don't believe I would have even contemplated publishing a book if it hadn't been for her. I'm just so grateful for her promptings and total willingness to help with anything.

Table of Contents

Paeroa

We've been in Paeroa now nearly two years
Really don't miss Auckland apart from the free beers
'Cause I worked in a brewery for a while
And the free beer allocation did make my husband smile
We love it in Paeroa because
Being retired now, it's made us pause
And realise what is important to us
It's not buying things or making a fuss
Our lives now are peaceful and uncomplicated
Retirement to us was totally underrated
We can work in the community and help people out
And make a small difference, there is no doubt
So, thank you Paeroa, for welcoming us here
It's the best decision we ever made that year

New Neighbours

When Nick gets home, it's not hard to tell
As his cattle truck leaves a rich rural smell
There's Bob, retired, across the way
His agapanthuses are his bug bare
He wanders around them every day
And tops any buds that dare to appear

Then we have Allen on the top side
He has lots of land rover wrecks he tries to hide
Tucked down the side of the fence
Amongst other junk and weeds so dense

John and Sue live at the back, Sue's mum passed away this
Christmas gone by
She'd just had a triple bypass; they didn't expect her to die
Sue collects bears; she has hundreds it would seem
I have one here, maybe he could join her team?
Gary and son, Matt, live down the right of way
Oh, and Nick, the cattle truck driver, is Gary's son, I forgot to
say
Matt is a quadriplegic; he has helpers coming in all day
It must be hard for him, but it's the only way

He has no movement from his neck down
But he always has a smile, never a frown

Myreen is up the other road, she's not long moved in
She took some of the yellow daisies I was putting in the bin
I nearly forgot there's Jill and Bruce, Chris and another Sue
They all live up our way too

And today I've met Melody, she lives three doors down
She has settled here from out of town
With her spotty dog she often goes walking
I stopped to have a pat, that's how we got talking.

Summer

The lawns have been mowed, they look really great
'Twas a very hot job done by my mate
They grow so fast even though there's no rain
I don't know why, but it is such a pain

The edges are done, and the garden is weeded
A good daily watering is now needed
It's a delight to see the flowers so bright
And the new added gardens complete the sight

Actually, there're still more gardens to come
And the bed for the bulbs is now nearly done
But alas! We are not happy when the temperature is high
And then when it's wet and windy, we sigh

We must learn to be happy, whatever the case
Whether it's sun, wind, or rain in our face

Church Welcome

Welcome, welcome here today, old and new
We're looking forward to spending this time with you
We hope you will feel the love and care
That surrounds everyone that is here
Our prayer is that you will be blessed today
And if you have any concerns at the end, let us pray
Our lesson on James will continue after praise
As we learn a lot more about his ways
Please linger around a bit at the end
For tea and coffee and sharing to spend

No Rain

As the sun slowly fades and day turns into night
The sky turns into a vivid delight
The birds quieten down and the temperature cools
And the frogs start calling in what's left of the pools
Because the temperature has been so high
All that one can do is hydrate and sigh
But the rain will come again one day soon
I think it has something to do with the moon
Then maybe we can sleep well again
As the temperature drops with the arrival of rain

Sounds of the Night

As the afternoon light starts to fade
And the low evening sun creates more shade
The birdies squawk as they fly off to roost
And the noise from the trees gets an incredible boost
They jostle and fight to find some space
That will be their special roosting place

The crickets make themselves well heard
And with the cicadas the racket is quite absurd
I hear the magpies give their last cry of the night
As they also look for a place that's just right

There's barking down the street, a small dog
Oh no! We have captured in our trap, a hog
Luckily only by its toes
So, we release it quickly and away it goes

Then the noise quietens down, there's an owl hooting out
there
His frantic mating call is filling the air
A delivery truck roars up the road every night
To the rest-home to leave his load, I think that is right

As we drift off to sleep, listening to the rain
The roar of a motorbike awakens us again
So, we toss and turn and talk a bit
The wariness has gone now, damn it!

Gus

We know this great guy called Gus
He now drives the big school bus
He has a jolly smile when the kids get on
But if they're noisy and rude that won't last for long
Don't misbehave or make a fuss
While Gus is driving the big school bus

Sometimes up the wrong road, he goes
And the frustration on his face sure shows
He has to back out if he can't turn around
There're probably a few new words he has found

He's missed the odd pickup stop
And yelling from the kids he does cop
Oh well! He'll drop them off on the way back
And he hopes that won't get them a smack

But he's admired for taking this on, from us
As he drives around the big school bus
Oh Gus, Oh Gus, what a character you are
As you drive the bus instead of your car

The Fall

I fell off my bike the other day
It hurt a fair bit as there I lay
Blood was running down my face from a cut above my eye
I was only going at a slow pace, but still, there I had to lie
While I got myself together again
And hopped on my bike despite the pain
I think damaged most was my pride
As we headed home and completed the ride

The Bike Ride

A new day has dawned, bright and clear
There's an autumn crispness in the air
It's off we go now to the cycle track
Me in the front and Ken at the back
He lets me go ahead and set the pace
I don't mind really as he can't see the grimace on my face

We wind our way through the shady glades
Over rough cattle stops that dislodge our shades
There's no wind today, just a gentle breeze
But some of the hills get you in the knees
And the bum that sure gets sore a bit
So, we're very tentative when next we sit

Nearly 22 kilometres we've done today
And when we get home that's where we'll stay
We're not as young as we used to be
A long ride like this takes it out of him and me
Maybe a nap will help us recover
There will no doubt be some new aches, we will discover
We'll do it all the next day again
You would think that we really enjoyed the pain

Hopefully the kilos will drop away,
As we go out for our ride every other day.

24

40 Years

'Twas 40 years ago I said
To Ken, I think it's time we wed
We'd lived together 3 years or so
And if I'd left it up to him, I know
We would still be in that same place
And I would not have had a happy face

So, take Friday off, as work's a bit slow
And down to the registry office we will go
No one knew what we did that day
And when we rang the families, they were all away

We went to the Pizza Hut for our wedding feast
And we had pizza and a carafe of wine at least
So happy we were when we went back to our home
The families we tried again to phone
Oh well! They would find out in due course
As we knew this one wouldn't end in divorce
Still happy and smiling we are to this day
And I'm sure to the end it will stay this way

The Park

I walk through the park with the big gnarly trees
And their beautiful long limbs sway in the breeze
They've been there a long time, I'm told
Some are well over 100 years old
When the strong summer winds come on by
Lots of branches are ripped off and die
But the birds in the vicinity love these trees
As they gently swing and sway in the breeze
They build lots of nests, the boughs are just right
Then they come back here and roost at night
There are large monkey puzzle trees, they give the park a charm
But look out when they shed, the pods may do you harm

Seasons of Life

I see your beauty everywhere
Through every season of the year
Your creations are a sight to see
From the highest mountain to the smallest tree

Spring brings new life to the dull winter shades
As the bitter winter wind slowly fades
The beauty of flowers that were hidden away
Fill the air with their fragrance during the day

As the long days of summer are hot and dry
The luscious green pastures wither and die
The hibiscus burst forth in colours so bold
With its intricate petals edged in fine gold

Then the days get shorter as autumn abounds
And the splendour of colour in the leaves is found
The beauty is there for us all to see
As the last autumn leaf hangs onto a tree

It then gets cold, oh so cold
We wrap up warm as the shorter days unfold
Maybe a frost tonight, that would be nice
And we wake in the morning to a landscape of ice
But the day will be cool, clear, and bright
As the sun sparkles off the frost, it's such a great sight

When the winter winds come and blow with such might
It's hard to sleep, another restless night
Then it's spring again – another year has begun
In the seasons of life, it's just another one

Calves

It's that time of year again
When the bobby calves feel the pain
Their mournful cries fill the night
To remind us of their terrible plight
There's nothing we can do for you now
You'll have to hope you can become a cow
You'll be raised and cared for another way
But in the open fields, you'll be unable to play
So, cry no more, don't break your hearts
Unfortunately, this is just how your life starts

Bugs in Garden

Cicadas grub, I'm sorry to disturb your life
If the birdies come, you'll soon be in strife
But in this soil, I need to dig
To extend my garden, not too big
Mr Worm is somewhere in there too
But he's OK because he makes lots of poo
Not too keen on the spiders there
I'll wear a hat, so they won't get in my hair

Hospital Waiting

There's a lady across the seat from me
It's a terrible sight to see
Her rolls of fat are nearly at her feet
And she sits there doing nothing but eat
She has dirty grey hair, it's on her chin too
I bet she has trouble having a poo
I don't know what she's here for today
But she surely needs some fat taken away

The Physio

I sit in the car while Ken's at the physio
If it's doing any good, we don't really know
There are exercises to do, he does them well
Every second day he gives them a spell

We're lucky if close to the clinic we can park
We often go around the block, it's a bit of a nark
Then occasionally a close space will appear
Oh good, we say, we'll park right here

It only takes half an hour or so
Then after a coffee, back home we will go
And next week, we will do it all again
Just hoping that all this will relieve his pain

Autumn

As the summer warmth fades away
The autumn colours make a bold display
There's orange, gold, copper and, of course, red
As the leaves on the trees are now being shed

We take a bit longer to get out of bed in the morn
Although we are still waking up at the crack of dawn
I lie there a bit as it's cool outside
Until I get a gentle shove on the backside

It's time to get up and get some things done
Then we can bike ride and have some fun
Now we have soups, they're real yummy too
And at night, sometimes, there'll be a stew

The afternoon sun fades away fast
With long shadows over the hills, it casts

Tapora

The morning chorus is early again
It's another stunning day, no sign of rain
There are all sorts of birds singing out there
Their chirping and cheeping does fill the air

The boys are setting the net today
And maybe do some fishing while away
Then when the tide recedes some more
We'll do some surfcasting from the shore

Over the mud flats we'll tramp to get to our spot
Maybe today, we might just get a lot
But really, it's fun just being out there
If we do or don't catch, we really don't care

There's plenty of walking to be done
But whatever we do, it's all good fun
As to be up here at Tapora, away from the noise
It's great to have a holiday with the boys

So, there's me and Ken, Rex and Gail
To enjoy ourselves, we never fail
And should it rain, we don't mind that too
As there's plenty of other things to do

I now hear a mozzie around my feet
Think it must be time for my breakfast to eat

The Hibiscus Flower

Oh Lord! What a magnificent sight to see
The hibiscus flower upon that tree
With dark large red petals shining so bold
All tinged with a hint of delicate gold
Even the back of the flower its beauty does display
And the yellow tips of its stamen splendour in slender array
If I were a bee, I couldn't pass it by
Its beauty is a beacon to catch the eye
To create such beauty is a triumph to behold
As with many other creations that unfold

The Birds

Oh! What a joy it is to see
All the wax eyes in the tree
Twittering just above my head
As they anxiously wait to be fed

The sparrows are there too not quite so bold
As they await their turn, fluffed up in the cold
And the mynahs, what pests they are
They seem to appear from near and far

But they're fun to watch, they're too big to get in
No matter how hard they try, they'll never win
They peer in the cage and stalk all around
Then they squawk in a rage and fly down to the ground

Go and annoy someone else I say
As I run outside and chase them away

Church

As I sit in church today
I wonder what the preacher will say
From the pulpit he says "Welcome here"
And let us know if you need a prayer
Were there any birthdays this week?
We wait in silence, no one prepared to speak
Oh yes, there was! How could we possibly forget
So up to the front they go, their chocolate bar to get
The lesson on James is interesting too
On all the trials and tribulations, he went through
The singing is glorious, it fills the air
If you sang out of tune, no one would care
Tea and coffee are available at the end
And time to catch up with a friend
There's a wonderful feeling of camaraderie and love
I'm sure it's all directed down from above

I Remember

I remember the days when we were young
Life was full of adventure and lots of fun
We'd be up early to muster the sheep
And wander the hills still half-asleep
Then off to school, a mile walk to the bus
With our marmite sandwiches, there was no fuss
Then ambling home, as there was still work to do
Chopping wood and gardening too

On the weekends, up early then out the door
To the back of the farm, there were places to explore
There were creeks to dam and turkeys to chase
Our lives were lived at a frantic pace
Sometimes it was rabbits we would dig out of their holes
As they leave the hillside like it had been attacked by moles
The rabbits were pests, they had to be killed
But to do this I was not particularly thrilled

We were all given spades, there were thistles to chop
And until the paddock was finished, we were not to stop
On the way home, eeling we would do
We always managed to catch one or two

Also, fair game would be a young kid
We'd chase it around and down the hills we would skid
Cuddling it close, we'd take it home, me and my brother
And Dad would growl, "Take that back to its mother."

If the weather was good and the tides were right
We'd go off to the beach for fish and mussels for dinner that night
The beach went for miles, it was a great place to be
We'd wander for hours and pick up beach debris
Sometimes glass floats would be just lying there
They'd come loose off fishing boats from somewhere

One day I noticed a bottle with a message inside
My excitement, I was not able to hide
I quickly took the message out to read
But it wasn't in English, but another creed
I had it translated but can't remember what it said
I'm afraid with age that memory is dead

We all had bikes, we would ride to our mates
Over metal roads and through farm gates
Sometimes it would rain, and we'd get so wet
And often an annoying puncture we would get
It was a long way home if that happened to us
As we were out in the sticks, there was no bus

We would make ourselves trolleys and race down the hills
And as you can imagine, there were plenty of spills
With broken arms and sometimes a bleeding head
We'd hurry home to Mum, some tears to shed

The nearest doctor was an hour and half away
So, the other kids at the neighbours' place would stay

I also remember cracked skulls and chopped toes
It was just the way life in the country goes
We all seem to survive, though sometimes I wonder how
When I think of these things, looking back now

Haymaking was to be done and shearing too
Never a shortage of work to do
The large country garden always had veggies to grow
And flowers to tend for the competitions to show
It was always fun at the Mardi Gra and fair
They held this in the district somewhere each year

The animals would be judged to see who would be best
And often we won, we had beaten the rest
The blooms on show were a delight to see
We'd wait in anticipation as to who the winner would be
The boys entered the slippery pig and another game
One of them won a duck, Petunia was her name
They took her home; they'd had so much fun
And built her a pond in the hen run

Oh, how life was so good in those days
It developed us to who we are in many ways
We learnt independence and many life skills
We were energetic and positive and had strong wills

And then I remember being sent far away
To boarding school – four years I would stay
And my first roommate that I met
She was crying and so upset
Being away from her parents broke her heart
But I couldn't wait for the adventure to start

The first day at assembly is engraved in my mind
Out of 1300 girls not one I knew could I find
That was the first time I'd really felt alone
And I remember looking around with a small inner groan

We used to sneak out into town or the beach
It wasn't too far and well within reach
We had to be careful as the Matron was tough
If we'd been caught, our lives would have been rough

We had Saturday night dances with the Boys High who were
not far away
The Matrons patrolled the grounds to ensure out of trouble we
would stay
No hanky panky allowed while they were around
So, we left the dances still safe and sound

I played lots of sport, I loved to compete
It was a great way for me, new people to meet
There was netball, tennis, and softball too
It was much more fun than the schoolwork to do

But I couldn't wait to leave and to make my own way
To get a good job and make lots of pay
And I remember my first flat – a little bungalow
Then into a flat with two other girls I would go

And oh, how we partied many a long night
To see ourselves the next morning was a terrible sight
But we survived the rigours of our younger life
And managed to grow up without too much strife
As the years roll by and many adventures unfold
There are still many more stories to be told

Lud

You were such a cutie pie
No doubt the apple of your mothers' eye
Those gorgeous curls and dimples too
I bet all the ladies just drooled over you
Lud, we've only known you such a short time
But your love for people does really shine
Being your and Val's neighbour was so much fun
We loved your cheeky banters when gardening was done
But it's new neighbours now to share a baking treat
It appears that their taste buds are just as sweet
So happy 80th birthday, Lud, it's a great milestone
We feel privileged to be your friends, I'm sure we are not
alone

Occasional Table

I'm a sexy brown colour and made of wood
I'd be more helpful if I could
They spread out puzzles on my back to do
And I've even seen a mouse or two

The carpet is warm beneath my feet
And there have been lots of wonderful people to meet
I talk to the African Violets near here
And other plants in the room elsewhere

My back gets rubbed nearly every week
I'd let them know how nice that was if I could only speak
When the sun filters through and warms my bones
If you listen hard, you'll hear gentle moans
The rubbish on TV is nothing to see
So, I'll just sit here quietly, being me

Holiday

On holiday we finally go
Way down south to see some snow
From the plane a patchwork of green is in the fields below
As the meandering streams out to the ocean flow

The rugged snow-capped peaks are standing proud
With some high and mighty ones covered in cloud
The flight was good, but Queenstown was wet
We were pleased into our rooms, to finally get

The next day dawned bright and clear
Up early for a walk I was in the crisp morning air
Just the odd puffy cloud drifted our way
But we had to move on, we weren't going to stay

On the winding roads to Arrowtown we went
For a quick hello, as more time tomorrow would be spent
The road to Wanaka was windy and steep
As we hoped no crazy drivers to meet

The ravages of winter had now long past
And the new growth of spring has arrived at last
Brilliant blossoms were such a sight to see
All, no doubt, hoping to attract many a bee
Every piece of flat land appeared to be
Planted in vines or some type of fruit tree

Barren, rugged hillsides reached up to the sky
They seemed almost endless as we passed them by
Every now and then, a brilliant touch of green
In the irrigated paddocks could be seen
We battled the wind on day three
Not a good day to be a bee
You could hardly stand against its incredible force
For this time of year, it's expected of course

The hillsides of schist create a dark hazy hue
And contrast the skyline with its deep shades of blue
The fickle spring weather has hit us again
As we wake up on day four to snow and rain
There are excited children playing in the yard
By mid-morning, it's snowing really hard

The snow was the first seen by some
But driving into town was certainly no fun
Heavy laden branches hung low in the still air
Birds still came out to feed, they didn't care
Now it's brightening up and the suns breaking through
Maybe we'll get out as there's plenty to do

The beauty around us took our breath away
Snow piled high on the roadsides as we headed out the next
day
The sky was clear, and a cold wind blew
They'd be a lot more amazing sights to see, we just knew
We travelled North through forests of rich dark green
And steep barren hills where the snow had been
A quick stop at Haast for something to eat
We sat in the sun, relishing its heat

Then up the coast in land with the mountains still in sight
We decided to stay at Fox Glacier for the night
Up early the next morning, some more sights to see
Lake Matheson was first, and still a bit chilly
The blackness of the lake made an incredible reflection
With the snow-capped mountains in the distance, I have
already mentioned
Franz Joseph glacier, our next stop on the way
We meandered a while over gravel paths, but we didn't stay

We whizzed around Ross, there wasn't much there to see,
An ice-cream on the way out, our memory of Ross would be
On to Hokitika, to stay a day or two
And to catch up with a nephew, there was plenty to do
You could hear the ocean roar as it pounded its might
A comforting sound to lull us to sleep at night

Although the car had a modern GPS
We still managed to be confused and get in a mess
But it didn't really matter, we had time to spare
So, if we ended up somewhere else, we didn't really care

Greymouth was next with many short stops on the way
To gaze in awe at rugged coastline clothed in sea spray
The sand flies were huge and hungry too
I think I was the only one they were attracted to

An old man on the breakwater stopped to talk
He hobbled along with his old dog, hardly able to walk
An old seadog, he used to be
With some harrowing tales of life at sea
Then off up the coast we continued our drive
Eventually in Nelson, we were to arrive

A day or two here to have a good look around
The boys were excited as a car museum we found
Then off on the plane back to Hamilton again
And thankfully, arrive safely and no further rain

Mum

Although my Mum's been gone quite a while
I still remember her beautiful smile
When I look back now, how little I knew
About the struggles in life, she went through
When she first married, it was tough starting out
With Dad at war and for two years not about
She lived with her parents as their first child had arrived
And kept herself busy to be a good mother, she strived

They moved several times once Dad was home from the war
And in a short time, the children numbered four
Two more were to arrive in the next few years
It was certainly a challenge, there were many tears
When Dad got his farm, they settled way out back
He took Mum and the children to live in a shack
What a shock to Mum to be this far out
With six children under eight running about
The water she carried from the creek
This life certainly was not for the meek
I wish I'd talked to her about these days
I think they affected her mentally in many ways

She couldn't cope and left us for a while
It would be a couple of years before we would again see that
smile
My memory of her was her being very tired
As I know at night times, she often cried
As children we helped whenever we could
From cooking meals to chopping wood
We did the gardens, lawns and baking too
We worked hard as there was always plenty to do
Mum taught music and loved her art
She played in an accordion band; it calmed her heart
She would take off for weeks with her art friend
Up creeks and into little known places, time they would spend
The inspiration from these trips was plain to see
And soon new images on canvas, there would be
Light opera she loved and with Dad they would go
To Pukekohe many nights to be in a show

When Dad sold the small farm, they moved out of town
To Te Puke with Grandma in tow they settled down
Our visits were short, only a few hours we would stay
Then after helping them and having lunch, we would be on
our way
Mum now had cancer and a breast had to go
She battled this bravely and if in pain, you'd never know
She changed her diet, exercised, and decided to fight
Eleven years more she had, but try as she might
There was no way to stop it, the cancer took hold
It moved quickly through her body; the end was near, she was
told
Her one regret, she told me one day when things were tough

Was she never told her children how much she loved them enough?
I think we never doubted her love for us
But that was just Mum's way, not to make a fuss
The suffering and pain would very soon cease
She knew her journey would lead her to peace
How often it is when someone close passes on
That we realise the life stories not told are now forever gone

The Assignment

The next assignment we are given to do
Is why we joined, I'll ponder on this a moment or two
Being new to Paeroa and just starting to write
There's a lot to learn, and there, I just might
I like to write on everyday things
Real life stories and the challenges it brings
An idea will come in the dead of night
Then there's no way to sleep, try as I might
I have to get up and put my ideas down
Then maybe drift off again until dawn comes around

Writing my dad's story was my longest one yet
Twelve pages in total, so we won't forget
Of the struggles they had in those early days
And how it directed our lives in many ways
I've written about my mum; it was a sad tale to tell
Because I left home early and did not know her well
The trips we've been on have not escaped my pen
And I'm sure there'll be more with my husband, Ken

Each granddaughter at Christmas received a poem last year
With words of encouragement and how much we care
That they seek wisdom from their parents and show kindness
to all
And that there will be challenges and sometimes they will fall
But the love of their family will always be there
To offer support no matter when or where

I've written of new neighbours as we moved house last year
But we haven't forgotten our old ones since we moved away
from there
And the delight in a garden full of colour and smell
I am amazed how the plants grow so well

Sometimes I ponder on what will happen when I'm gone
And hope that my poetry may continue to live on
Maybe someone somewhere will enjoy what I write
Maybe, just maybe, someone just might

Aunty Peter

Peter, our aunt, our favourite one
We knew if you were there, there'd be lots of fun
We took you out fishing, it was such a blast
But those poor ageing arms were not up to the task
A squeal of delight when a fish took your bait
"Simon, I need you, your fish can wait"
Although our visits were too few, I hate to say
You were often in our thoughts in a very special way
Now you're at peace, you'd just had enough
A blessing for you, for your family it's tough
Goodbyes are not forever; goodbyes are not the end
They simply mean we will miss you until we meet again

Best Mates

It's been an interesting journey coming to Best Mates
From the adorable Tama to the disappearing plates
There's Sally who, like a trooper, does swear
And cross Melissa at your peril if you dare

Mel rules the office, and with her eagle eye
She will spot any mistake and ask you why
Sam is here, we call him "Give me Five"
As he flies around the place like a bee in a hive

And Donut Dean who munches his way
Through swathes of lollies and cakes each day
About David and Amir, what can I say
Just that it's good that they live so far away

Be patient with Glynis, there's a lot for her to learn
And you certainly don't want another to struggle and burn
Oh, there's many more characters, and I love you all
And I'm going to stop now before I bawl
Thank you, Best Mates crew, I hope that in some way an impact I've mad
As time rolls on and your memory of me will gradually fade.

Easter Thursday

The angry crowd roars louder, they're moving so slow
I see a person surrounded, but who? I do not know
A feeling of dread is consuming me
Why have they all come, what will I see?
I'm following the crowd, there's anguish in the air
My heart is heavy, but I know not what to fear
Where are YOU, Lord? What is taking place?
I climb up a tree and catch a glimpse of his face
They're dragging you with a crown of thorns on your head
What will become you, what lies ahead?
The promises you made, Lord, with the bread and the wine
Surely, surely, these will still be mine?
I can hardly bear to watch what is happening here today
But I must as I'm mesmerised, as the crowd passes this way
Surely, you've not been betrayed, who would do this to you?
And I trudge with hunched shoulders with the crowd to see
what they'll do

Grey Silk Bag

Little grey silk bag, I wonder what you are for?
Lying so alone and crumpled on the floor
What gems have you held? What secrets do you hold?
If only you could speak, what stories could be told?
Was it a diamond you cushioned that sparkled so bright?
That dazzled and shone when held to the light
Or an emerald so bold and brilliantly green
The colour was so rich as never before had been seen
Maybe a sapphire or amethyst? Who would know
What precious jewel was tied up with a bow?
Perhaps not a gem had been held in your care
But just a memory of someone held dear
A piece of jewellery from someone who had passed
And kept in here forever to last
So little grey silk bag, I do hope you'll find
The person who treasured you and left you behind

The Jones'

The Jones, Roger, Annie and family, your friends are gathered here today
To say farewell to you, as you have moved away
There is no doubt and I'm sure all will agree
How blessed your new community will be
For the commitment you made, we can't thank you enough
As you juggled your farm life, at times it must have been tough
When the need arose, you would always be there
And never a negative word did anyone hear
Your croquet rules, Roger, were a mystery to behold
And some stories about that should remain untold
But we've had some great times and our memories we'll treasure
You have brought much happiness, much more than we can measure
Be safe in your endeavours, whatever they may be
And expect many visitors for a cup of Earl Grey Tea
You have a dream to follow, we're very excited for you
We hope you'll enjoy your new life and be happy in all that you do

Love and Cherish

I chose the words 'love and cherish' today
As the other two are not really in my life in any way
For me, to love is a heartfelt thing
It comes from the heart like an eternal spring

I have different levels of love in my life
There's a very deep love in being a wife
There's love of family and friends that's not quite so deep
But still in my heart a place to keep
I just love the life that's been given to me
And that's another level of love to see

It's a curious thing, this thing called love
It cannot be seen, it must come from above
But in saying that, it would be true to say
That love can be shown in many a different way

Now to cherish, that's something entirely different, again
It will give you delight and comes with no pain
There are a few things I cherish, I must say
I really cherish the freedom of the life I have today

To be able to live a fulfilled life that is stress free
And to have a healthy loving husband still living with me
I cherish my childhood and the memories that brings
And I cherish each bird in the morning that sings

There are just so many things in life I feel
That the words 'love and cherish' to me are very real

Mates

It really was so great the way
They always found something to talk about
It's not like they met every day
But what they said had plenty of clout
Many a problem they could share without fear
And solve with some knowledge from yesteryear
They could huddle for hours discussing this and that
These deep discussions never ending in a spat
They talked of lost dreams and loves that had past
Their friendship was strong, they knew it would last
When everyone around was passing them by
Their truly blessed friendship would last 'til they'd die
Never a bad word was said of anyone
They just enjoyed their time together and had lots of fun
And at the end they would just sit, neither able to speak
Their life was nearly over, they were now very weak
One night they let go, nothing more could they say
They would now have to meet in some other way

The New Pastor

We have a new Pastor come our way
His name is Bryce, we hope he will stay
His flock are eager for his teachings to hear
And his messages of encouragement come loud and clear

He has a love of burgers, not that you can tell!
It must have been tough during the lockdown spell
His youth and enthusiasm are obvious to see
I'm sure to the Church, a great asset he will be

And of course, his lovely wife, Carol, a woman of God
Who will be there to support and guide and give him the nod
To be part of this community is a privilege indeed
They will gladly accept you if God's promptings you heed

So, we welcome your family into this new pastoring ground
May you find blessings in many things not yet found
Continue in the journey God has now set out for you
You're here for a reason and there's plenty for you to do

Farewell Drop in Centre

Old bossy britches Hui, said I had to do
A farewell poem and read it out to you
"Not sure I can," I said in protest
But here it is, anyway, I've done my best

What a privilege it has been to share
Some time with others who really care
The characters I've met have touched my heart
And although I'm leaving, the memories won't part

Doug's scones will be missed, they are so fine
I hate to admit it, but they're much better than mine
The laughter and stories I will miss too
But it's time in my life, other things to do

So, for me there's exciting times ahead
Even though it will be early out of bed
I'll be off to Matamata early each day
To the market gardens, I'll make my way

I'll administrate production of the growing of crops
Veggies, that is, definitely not hops
My office will vary between two places
I'll have to get my brain into gear to remember new faces

So, it's goodbye from me for a while anyway,
And I think that's really all that I've got to say

Mr Scrooge

Now Mr Scrooge loved his bike-stand which stood proud and
tall
Propped up in his garage against the far wall
And because he was such a miserly fellow
He'd painted it with paint he had, which of course was yellow

It was very unique this bicycle-stand
As it folded up and he took it with him on trips he had planned
When he heard the America's Cup racing was on
He hopped on his bike, and he was gone

Into town he rode with his bicycle-stand in tow
There was no way he was going to miss this show
He took some large inflatable tyres he had made
Attached them to his bike and into the water did wade

On his transformed bike he peddled his way
Out on the harbour where the America's Cup boats were to
play
But the wind got up and it started to rain
He just made it back; he'd not do that again

So, he deflated the tyres and put his regular ones back
Picked up his yellow bike stand and returned to his shack

Stunt Woman

Far in the distance, I could see
A tiny speck, moving slowly towards me
An adventure I was going on today
To meet the cement ship coming into the bay

The runabout we were in was going to meet
This big ship, but not just to greet
An inspector and pilot on board, we had
To check that the skipper was doing no bad

They'd asked if I would like to go along too
"You bet," I said, "what a fun thing to do"
As the ship drew nearer, we slowed our speed
And drew alongside, a steady hand they would need

Down to nine knots we had both slowed to now
The pilot went first to show me how
So, with camera secure, on the edge, I would stand
And grab hold of the rope ladder with my left hand
The breeze came up, the ladder twisted and turned
I hung on tight, and my knuckles burned

But up to the deck, I arrived with a sigh
An adrenaline rush, I was on a high

I felt like a stunt woman, the thrill was insane
Then the clouds thickened up and it started to rain
We chugged up the harbour, it was a beautiful sight
The skipper on board had done everything right
We docked at the wharf and back to the office I went
It had been one of the most exciting days in a long while I had
spent

Carrots (Bugs Bunny)

Oh, how I love the Wilcox carrots, they really are so sweet
I hop into the paddocks and eat and eat and eat
I tell my friends, they join me too
I guess it's just what a rabbit needs to do
But when they're gone, my eating habits will have to change
I guess I'll just look around for another range

Waharoa

My new workplace in Waharoa is draughty and cold
It gets even worse in the winter, I'm told
But the workmates there make it a welcoming place
This more than makes up for any discomfort I may face
The old house stands in paddocks of salad greens and broccoli too
I love the environment for my new work I must do
There's comradery in the team, they work very hard
They don't seem to mind the dust and mud in the yard
Sometimes the crop picking cannot go ahead
I don't think they mind, as it's more time in bed
We're hounded by flies, their buzzing won't cease
But now with some dispensers, we may get some peace
We get broccoli to take home when that picking is done
The heads are huge and there's plenty for everyone
I love going to work in the rumpty old house
I couldn't imagine doing anything else

Christchurch March 2019

Through grief, our different faiths collide
But our hearts of love we will not hide
Your pain we feel, I'm sure you know
And we pray for you in the candle glow

Do not fear, your lives to live
From now on our love, we will give
We'll look out for each other every day
That this will never happen again, we pray

Mourn for your loved ones as we do too
But gain strength from love to see you through
Together as Kiwis, we will stand strong
Although we know your pain will never be gone

Life Changes

As soon as he walked into the room
He knew his life was about to change forever
The air was filled with tragedy and gloom
An atmosphere he had experienced before, however
This time, though, it would mean much more
As the solicitor quietly closed the door
Your father has died, his business is now yours
He looked up for a moment in a silent pause
You'll have to take over as soon as you can
Even though you have no idea how his business ran
I'll give you a week to think about what to do
And how you move on, it will be up to you
He knew so little of what his father did
Only that it was successful, he certainly made a quid
So that was the end of his own career now
He'd have to make some difficult choices somehow
The business was too good to let it slip
There were already goods waiting that needed to ship
Once the shock had worn off, he would endeavour
To live his new life that would change forever

Ponderings

Sometimes I lie in bed and ponder
When I pass, will anyone miss me? I do wonder
Will they say I lived a fulfilled life?
Or did I cause many moments of strife?
Will they say I was caring and helpful too?
Or did I just do what I needed to do?
Will they remember someone who got things done?
And loved to explore and have lots of fun
Will they remember a gardener so keen?
Who loved to plant flowers for all to be seen
Will they remember a close friend to a few?
But friendly to all those that she knew
Will they remember those she helped on the way?
To lighten their load and have a great day
Will they remember a generous soul?
Who would bake you a cake or a casserole
Will they remember someone who struggled each day with pain?
But tried to hide it and never complained
Maybe for a short while they'll remember me
But the memories will fade quickly, that's OK, just how it will be

Because there's nothing too amazing in my life that I've done
Nothing to trigger long memories for anyone
Maybe in death, though, my poems will live on
Long after the other memories have faded and gone

75

Promptings

The first sounds of dawn hailed the new day
With every shrill and tweet, they just seemed to say
Get out of bed, you've got things to do
You never know what might happen, who you will bump into
For some strange reason, hard to say why
I had an excited expectation, to understand it I wouldn't even try
At 10 am, the landlady turned up, not unexpected though
She wanted to say thank you and had a large gift basket in tow
Then off to the Drop-in Centre some games with friends to play
This is such a fun place where lonely people for a few hours can stay
We then headed off to Thames and decided to stop and see
The cafe at Matatoki, what a delight that would be
I said to the Cafe owner, I thought I knew her from somewhere
She said she'd moved down from Auckland, I said, I was also from there
We talked a bit more then it came to me
That we had done pamper parties together for brides to be
Before we left, a couple was sitting there

They were cycling around New Zealand, they had lots of gear
"Where are you going to stay the night from here?" I said
"In Paeroa," they answered, "well then you must come to our
place for a bed"
"We're just off to Thames, we have some shopping to do"
So, if you call around after four, you can have a hot shower
too
"We can hear all about your travels and country over a meal
And show some Kiwi hospitality that is for real"
The couple were from Germany, three months they would be
here
Cycling throughout the country and stopping here and there
After a hearty breakfast early the next day
They hopped on their bikes and peddled away
Sometimes the promptings we receive, we choose to ignore
But if we act on these, we will be blessed even more
This was certainly the case on this Tuesday just gone
The blessings we received that day will forever live on

Mechanical Know-how

The little old lady sat in her car
By the look on her face, she was not going far
She turned the key, only a clunking noise was heard
She kept on turning the key, how absurd
Out she jumped with a hammer held high
Lifted the bonnet and let out a sigh
She banged and banged with that hammer so hard
I can only imagine how much her hand must have jarred
She opened the door and jumped in, and tried it again
The look on her face was anguish and pain
One more try with that hammer was in store
To get this engine running like before
"I like your mechanical prowess," I called out
And with a gummy grin she turned about
"I'm waiting for a new starter motor and have for a while"
As she hops back in the car with a fading smile
She turns the key in the ignition once more
And blow me down, the motor suddenly starts to roar
She threw the hammer back in the car
And headed away, thankfully she didn't have far

Philip

My brother Phillip is here today
I hope you will enjoy what he has to say
The second youngest of six is he
Which makes him just a tad older than me
He's travelled the world and done many a thing
So, some of his stories to you he will bring
I'm very proud of my brother, many a soul he's inspired
His life is lived at full pace, that's just how he's wired
So, sit back and enjoy the tale he will tell
And let your minds travel with him for a spell

Different Times

(An assignment from our writers group, using the words in bold)

In 1600, to James 1st was born a son

He was called **Charles 1st** by everyone

He married a princess, Henrietta of Bourbon

They had a daughter; he so wanted a son

A very disagreeable and pompous man was he

And ran a tyrannical absolute monarchy

He frustrated parliament with conflicts galore

Resulting in starting the English civil war

In 1949 at the age of forty-nine

He was beheaded as he would not resign

We now skip a couple of centuries to the **1800s,** no less

And even then, there was still conflict and the world in a mess

This era however was known for an invention boom

The escalator, the zipper, and the jacquard loom

There was barbed wire, Coca Cola, contact lens and much more

I could go on and on, but it would probably bore

Then one **Christmas** in **London** we were

Where the men all wore hats, and the ladies wore fur

But it was a Christmas like no other we'd ever had
The air was filled with sirens, you could tell it was bad
In bunkers below the smouldering earth, we hunkered down
It was cramped and smelly, and you could not move around

We could hear the Rolls Royce merlin engines of the spitfires
above
And wondered what was happening to those that we loved
Finally, the darkened sky became very still
Then the noise of people screaming, our ears would fill
We stumbled out of our bunker into the cool night air
And could only look with horror at the destruction there

Many years later, we called in on a friend
Rummaging in a shed, some time we would spend
An old **crankshaft** I spied, tucked away at the rear
"You don't want that," my husband said, "leave it here"
"No, no you're wrong," I said, "can't you just see
What a great garden ornament, this crankshaft would be"
"What's it from, where was it found?"
"It's from a crashed spitfire, and found buried in the ground"
Now it stands in my garden, a sight to behold
And a great story that will continue to be told

Alan and Glenys

Alan and Glenys, we are gathered here today
To bid you farewell, as you're going away
You'll probably never realise the inspiration you've been
And the lives you have changed with the people you've seen
You've nurtured and laughed and sometime shed a tear
But you always drew strength from your God that was near
You made the town your own and prayed for us all
Now you'll take a different direction, you've had that call
Whatever course your lives may now take
Be guided by God in the decisions you make
Take our love and our best wishes with you
We'll keep you in our prayers and in our hearts, too

Waiting in Line

Oh, the hours I must have spent
Waiting in line for some sort of event
The very first time, I remember it well
And it's a story today that I still tell
It was at primary school when the nurse came for the day
Jabbed us all, then went on her way
Three of my older brothers in the queue up ahead
Would faint on the ground as the needle they feared
I always thought it funny that I was the toughest one
And it gave me something to tease them about and have a bit
of fun

Then there was standing in line at a concert or show to see
Always excited anticipation in the crowd there would be
And you'd have to stand in line to go to the loo
Hoping you wouldn't have to do number two
We've stood in line at the airport to check in
With huge bustling crowds making a mighty din
There's been times at conferences that we've been to
You just have to stand there, there was nothing else to do

Sometimes we'd stand in line at the takeaway bar
And get sick of waiting and just sit in the car
So, as I ponder on this thing called 'waiting in line'
I guess it's always for something special, so that's just fine

84

The Drover – Jack

A story I was going to write
But it didn't work, try as I might
So, I've written it in poem instead
I hope you will enjoy it when read

In 1915, Jack was just a wee lad
Who later turned out to be my dad
The eldest of eight, *he'll follow my footsteps*, his father thought
But as he grew older, they often fought
To Jack, being an engineer, he couldn't stand
He'd always been driven to work on the land

So, at 17, after another row and his father's strike
He packed his bags and hopped on his bike
He rode and rode 'til he reached a friend's place
And no longer his father's wrath would he face
They gave him a share milking job and he earned his keep
Then he moved onto neighbours to work with their sheep
His family accepted he would never come back
They knew the stubbornness of their son, Jack

Life was tough back in those days
But to Jack it was great, he was learning new ways
He changed the way the farm was run
And worked long hours with little help from their lazy son
At haymaking time their son had a bad fall
And this then left Jack to handle it all
Thank goodness for helpful neighbours, they showed him
how to stack
But rounding the stack corner, he received a nasty smack

The pitchfork handle had swung around
And with his face covered in blood, he crashed to the ground
So, it was off to the dentist after that clout
And the dentist decided all the teeth must come out
All broken and cracked the teeth were in there
It would cost far too much for him to repair
Six months without teeth was not a good look
Especially when trying a date to book
With a gummy smile he would take his chance
And headed to town for the local dance
No luck that night, no lady to call
He'd just have to wait for some teeth, that's all
He played rugby and tennis, Jack loved his sport
In Taupiri, he helped locals establish a court

1934 and Gisborne was calling, a station with sheep
And horses to break in, that the owner would keep
90 unbroken horses were there to be tamed
He managed all that without getting maimed
This was a job he'd never before done
And not really his idea of having fun

Then the Māori shepherd and Jack were sent
To split rimu battens, six weeks were spent
5000 battens, the target that was set
It was the middle of winter, very cold and wet
The 8 ft saw was a mean gnarly thing
Even though it was cold, a sweat it would bring

Nearly finished the job and a big storm did blow
With freezing temperatures, driving sleet and snow
A big tawa tree was felled during the night
Destroying their camp, it was a frightening sight
They packed up their swags after a cold meal
Finishing the job as 5000 was the deal

Seven miles back to the station, to report to the boss
But the first river they reached looked impossible to cross
The Maori boy headed out tentatively to see
If he could tie a tight wire round a tree
The swags were across, now Jack's time had come
But by then the river had risen by some

Swept off his feet, he hung on for dear life
He finally made it, they were out of that strife
Both bitterly cold and wet right through
Keep moving fast, they knew they had to
Ice clung to their oilskins as they struggled up hills
To continue, regardless, was the strength of their wills

In a state of collapse, they finally reached home
And for a couple of weeks after, they didn't dare roam

Jack loved the station life, and he knew
No more share milking, as his passion for sheep farming grew
The boss had a grey mare, she was a great bucking horse
And while out moving stock, it was part of the course
She would buck Jack's boss off; he got hurt really bad
So, his boss said to Jack, "You can keep her, lad"
Jack loved this horse, for him she was gentle and calm
In all the years he rode her, she never once caused him harm

One day out with the boss's son
Moving a large mob of hogget's had to be done
Across a shallow creek, they all had to go
He failed to check why they were going so slow
400 sheep were smothered that day
Jack knew darn well what the farmer would say

The loss of these sheep to the farmer was a big blow
Out of the creek they dragged them to skin, he knew this job
was going to be slow
At least by doing this, not all was lost
But selling the skins hardly covered the cost
After a mighty row, the son left the farm
To a station up the coast, hopefully nothing else to harm

'Twas now 1936 and Jack had turned twenty-one
He spent six weeks in hospital with a bad back, that was no
fun
His sister took him home to give him some care
But an urgent call came from the old station, he was needed
up there
He was sent out the back some firewood to chop

Even with his sore back, he still wouldn't stop
The 10-horse pack carted it back
It was dropped at the homestead for him to stack
Then 5000 sheep, he'd have to shepherd alone
He just got on with it, he never did moan
He lived in a cottage, behind the homestead out the back
With his house cow and garden, there was little he did lack

Jack made his own bread and butter as well
Although life was hard, to him it was just swell
For 25 shillings a week, he virtually ran the show
And when he asked for a raise, the boss said, "You can go"
"But I'm doing everything here; it's not a lot to ask?"
So, the boss backed down, and agreed he was up to the task

Up the Mokonui Range, Jack was told to go
With 36 pack horses, it was his job, he couldn't say no
The horses had to be shod before making tracks
And 21 saddles were used with the packs
A big job it was, they would have to stay
At a local marae, they passed on the way
The marae lent them a paddock to use overnight
Next day was Christmas and what a delight,
Was the meal they were asked to share
There was a huge hangi and of course plenty of beer

What Jack needed now was a dog of his own
And one day through the camp, one did roam
He was eight weeks old, skinny, and shy
Not sure what he'd be like, but Jack gave him a try
After giving him a bath and making him clean

He rubbed all his skin with thick Vaseline
To get rid of the scabs and bugs that he'd had
As when he found him, he was a sorry sight and very sad
'Chief', he called him, he was the best and lots of fun
He even held his own in the sheepdog trial run

Now Jack loved his rugby, he played when he could
The wild pork, turkey and spuds after the games were real
good
The highlight of a game, I was told
Was the whiskey at half time to keep out the cold
Could you imagine if they did that today?
I'm sure the authorities would have something to say

Jack then moved on to a head shepherds' job
At a week's earning of two pounds five bob
After ten months, he moved on again
Managing 2000 acres and more experience to gain

Six miles up a muddy road and track
He arrived at this new home; it was just a shack
When he went inside the place, he was to stay
There was no electricity and the stove had rusted away
On an open fire, the cooking was done
Using a camp oven, he only had one

The nearest neighbour was seven miles away
Where he could collect mail and groceries on a Friday
Jack found the farm scrubby and rough
But in those days, the farm men were really tough

He killed wild pigs whenever he could
And lived on the pork, it tasted real good

There were wild cattle in the bush up there
And heavy woolled sheep he would have to shear
With hand shears, he got to work on those sheep
The wool was full of scrub and fern, no good to keep
A three day drove to the sale with the sheep
Meant several nights under the pines he would sleep
The joy of a shower when he arrived at the yards
And maybe a cold beer if he played right his cards
The shearing days were long and hard
And relief with the last sheep in the yard
They started at 5 am by candlelight
And worked each day, well into the night

Jack, now twenty-three, had managed so far
To get by without having a car
A 1919 Dodge he saw for 25 pounds
This would be great to get him around
"Could you teach me to drive?" he asked the man
"I've got a couple of spare hours, sure I can"
So, waiting around for some repairs they had to do
The owner came out and said, "The cop can test you at 2"

No time to think or even get scared
As he wasn't in any way for a test prepared
But off he went round the block and down a narrow lane
"You back yourself out of there, son, and your licence you
will gain"
Shaking like a leaf, he made it back

So, the cop handed the completed licence to Jack
"Not very confident, yet are you"
No surprise with what Jack had just gone through
A nerve-racking drive he had home that day
As the gears of the Dodge had plenty of play

Three months later in town, with shopping to do
The car dealer caught up and said, "I've got just the car for you"
A model A Ford, 2-seater, he took it for a whirl
With a big smile on his face, this would get him his girl
Now to pay the 85 pounds for his car
Jack knew he would have to drove stock afar
With 500 wethers and 390 bullocks they went on their way
It had rained very heavily all that day
They camped the night in a local farmer's shed
Where they were able to dry out and get themselves fed
The next day in heavy rain, they moved to the next stopping place
But another drover had beaten them, their animals filled the space

A farmer next door gave them a paddock on much higher ground
During the night the river had risen, 900 wethers of the other drover were drowned
They lost three of their dogs in the flood as well
The relief on Jack's face was easy to tell
Seven days it was before they could move on
By that time most of the water had gone

It was at this time the war had broken out
Jack joined the mounted rifles, so he could get about
A staff sergeant, he had become
And a large mob of horses, he would have to run
1300 horses had arrived to be trained and sorted
A contagious disease swept through them, and the camp was
aborted
870 horses were affected, 52 died
There was no way to save them as much as they tried

Life had now slowed somewhat for Jac
He had to get some excitement back.
So off with a mate to the local dance
When he first met Molly, it was love at first glance
He was invited home to meet her folks
They thought he wasn't such a bad bloke
Jack had to get work and get about
He knew he'd need money to take his girl out

With bullocks, bulls, and boner cows, he now was his own
boss
This would be tricky as they had the Fairfield Bridge to cross
The animals walked on until they came
To a driveway with a gate open – what a shame!
They headed up the drive, smashing a narrow gate down
There was an almighty loud crack; they knew Jack was in
town
Although they'd been warned a mob would come through
It wasn't Jack's fault if they chose nothing to do

The stock has right of way, everyone knew
But an impatient driver on the bridge honked his horn and startled a few
The stock bunched up in sudden fright
And pushed the guy's car over to the right
He clung onto the steering wheel with terror on his face
The beasts were in control, they knew their place

Another job he'd had to do
Was to move a dairy herd, there were quite a few
The road ran close to a railroad track
A train came along, and the cows bolted back
He rounded them up and moved on again
Hoping there'd be no other train

Jack needed a break, as the country was steep
He sat under a tree for lunch and then fell asleep
A train whistle woke him, gave him a hell of a fright
And when he looked around, no cows were in sight
The dogs knew their job, luckily for Jack
As the herd had been stopped just a little way back

His next job was a big one, 800 wethers to shift
He was tired, and while riding, in and out of sleep he did drift
Four days it would take, over the Fairfield Bridge again
The road was very wet and shiny with rain
It frightened the sheep; they were too scared to cross
As the traffic built up, Jack was at a loss
But some of the drivers hopped out and gave him a hand
He finally got them off the bridge and onto some land

There were many times during these days
Where the droves went by rail lines and the beast went their ways
But to work on his own, he had to do
He was very lucky, really, he only lost a few

Then in the paper for the air force he noticed an ad
The earlier training for this, he had had
It would fit in well for what they required
He thought a change might be good, so he applied

It was now 20 months since "Yes," Molly had said
So, they decided it was now time they were wed
Some of Jack's mates found what route they had taken
And turned up at their hotel for a celebration
They headed down to Blenheim, a bedsitter to share
It was very small and of furniture bare
But after three weeks, another transfer came
Rotorua, no married quarters, it was such a shame

Molly, for a while, went to her parents to stay
And Jack was sent overseas, far away
Two years deployment, it turned out to be
Then home at last, his new daughter to see

In the next few years, Jack's family grew
And now with young children, he had a few
His wandering days were now well over
He now was a farmer, no longer a drover
Just after the sixth, one (Sybil) was born
He heard his name from the farm ballot drawn

Jack was excited they'd have their own place
He had no idea all the trials he would face

With six children under the age of eight
To finally get their house was a two-year wait
They lived in a converted implement shed
Certainly not what Molly had envisioned when wed
There was no running water or any power
They washed in a big copper, there was no shower
The water was drawn from a nearby creek
This lifestyle was certainly not for the meek

The older children were homeschooled, there was no other way
And Jack, all his time spent breaking in the farm every day
There was a shed to be built and fencing to be done
To keep the horses and cows in the house run

With no animals yet and little to eat
Jack hunted wild goats to kill for meat
These years were tough, but they struggled through
There was really nothing else they could do
If they wanted this to be their dream place
They had to tough it out and put on a brave face

Jack was very active in the local neighbourhood
He set up committees and helped where he could
He organised a hall committee, monthly movies, table tennis and more
Jack relished being involved, it wasn't a chore

With years of farming and many a highs and low
He was getting old now and decided to go.
It was a hard decision, but it had to be done
Jack's three youngest sons said the farm they would run
They paid him out and he moved closer to town
To a small farmlet, so he could settle down
They finally ended up in a retirement home
Molly passed away early, then Jack was alone

At 92, Jack was then laid to rest
He'd had a good life; he'd given it his best

Ephesians 1

Paul wrote, our blessed God is the God of Glory
He reiterates this constantly throughout the Ephesians story
It's in Christ we really find out who we are
He's right here beside us, never far.

God's whole focus on us was love
He poured this down on us from above
Because of his sacrifice we are Abundantly Free
He gave us the way to be the best we could be

May your eyes be focused and clear
With the love of our God always present and near
He's in charge of the Universe and everything we know
Put your whole trust in him and your path he will show

The Church is Christ's body in which he speaks and acts
Just open your heart and believe in the facts

Ephesians 2

Oh, how sinful were my early days
Polluted with unbelief and wicked ways
God still covered me, he bided his time
I had no idea what he had in store for this life of mine

With mercy and love he embraced my life
And lead me away from a world of strife
And when my full attention he had
He showed me a better way, of which I am glad

He opened doors and new works I could do
I just had to listen to be shown the way through
He tore down the wall and rich promises made
He listened and guided me about things that I prayed

We all have come through this transition, it's clear,
And those old sinful ways are no longer near
Why would you not want to submit to his rule?
The life that he gives us is a real and precious jewel

Ephesians 3

God has made promises to one and all
Whether a non-believer or have heard the call
Paul's life work was to help people understand
To be open to the way that God had planned

Although Paul understood not what he was to do
He encourages us to travel by faith as God meant us to
When we trust in him, we're free to say what needs to be said
He's leading the way, he's one step ahead

Paul prays for a glorious inner strength to be found
We know God's teachings are pure and sound
God can do anything, far more than we know
So, open your hearts and minds, and the way he will show

Ephesians 4

I read and listen and try to see
What the message from the Lord in this passage can be
What's he really trying to say
Have I strayed from his word and lost my way?
But I feel I'm on track, but not nearly there
It will be a long journey, many a year
The peace this knowledge brings me, makes my life a joyful thing
Now to everyone I meet, this joy I must bring
So, to be like Jesus, our minds have to entwine
It may take a lifetime for our hearts to align
For us to finally put off our former, sinful ways
To our old worldly desires, we must daily reappraise
Our old lustful thoughts must daily be transformed
Our greedy attitudes will need to be reformed
Our minds have to be continuously changed
From our corrupt attitudes, we must become estranged
To be like Jesus, takes the Holy Spirit's doing
It may take a lifetime but it's so worth pursuing!

Ephesians 5

Out of respect for each other, reverent we must be
Not hidden or secret, but honest for all to see
Partners are not to dominate each other
But work and live in harmony, not smother
To love and cherish and not to tear down
To encourage a smile and not to frown
With love, teach your children to honour and respect
And to obey the rules that you expect
Build them up with encouragement and praise, whenever you
can
So, they will mature into a positive, well-balanced woman or
man
Don't hold onto your love, share it around
It's been given to you as a gift and is truly profound
Then what a glorious life you will get to live
But remember to accept love as well as to give

Ephesians 6

As Ephesians chapters come to an end
I reflect on the message the Lord wants it to send
To me he says: Put on God's armour, it will see you through
The many challenges in life that will come to you
Put on God's armour and don't be afraid
His sacrifice for your sins has already been paid
Put on God's armour and your life will be calm
When you read through God's word and many a psalm
Put on God's armour and although you're not immune from pain
The deep dark valleys will have no hold on you gain
Put on God's armour and tested you'll be
But know that he's there and sees what you see
Put on God's armour, it's there for us all
It's up to us now to answer his call
Put on God's armour, it will not weigh you down
It will lighten your load with a smile, not a frown

Penpals

Many years ago, when mum was at school
They were encouraged to write as a learning tool
There would be a list of students from afar
They could write to and find out who they are
My mum picked one from France, her name was Heléne
She liked the look of her by the pictures she'd seen
So, at 14 years old mum started to write
And when her first letter was replied to, it was such a delight
Although written in French, this would be her new mate
But she then had to find someone able to translate

They wrote about all the things that young girls often do
Things that they'd done and places they'd gone to
Then as they married, and their families grew
There were many more things to share with each other too
They would send over gifts of each country to see
And sent at Christmas, a New Zealand calendar there would
be
For 56 years they communicated as often as they could
Mum had a proper translator now, which was really good
The last letter to Heléne was from my Dad

It told of Mums' life and that she had passed, it was so sad
This was the last letter:

Dear Heléne,
Regretfully I am writing to tell you that your pen friend of 56
years Molly Woodward passed away early on Sunday
morning the 18th Sept. She had suffered a lot and had been on
morphine twice a day since April. She said a while ago that
she had accepted Jesus and was ready to go. We had fifty-one
years of marriage, love, and companionship. 180 people came
to her funeral from all the districts where we had lived. She
was well known for her music teaching and for her landscape
oil painting, and we had enjoyed taking part in Light Opera.
She leaves me, six children, twenty grandchildren and two
great grandchildren. I had always hoped that somehow you
would have been able to meet each other, but unfortunately it
was not to be.

Very sincerely,
Jack Woodward

But many years later, twenty-seven in fact
Heléne's youngest son, Patrick, has made contact
What a thrill it was one day to see his note
Asking if we were related to Molly, to whom his mother wrote
The family were clearing out the house Heléne lived in
And thankfully went through boxes before putting in the bin
There tucked away and kept for all those years
Were the letters mum had written, it nearly brought me to
tears
Heléne's family said they felt they knew us so well

And some of Heléne's past life they were happy to tell
We've now received copies of some of the letters Mum sent
And it's given us more knowledge of how her life was spent
Patrick the youngest is planning a trip to New Zealand next
year
They want to explore all the places Mum mentioned and held
so dear
It will be a great opportunity for our family too
To all get together again, as we so rarely do

Fog

It's not here yet, but it will surely come
As the dawn starts to appear and the night is done
Over the hills its wet tentacles do creep
As it slowly fills up all the valleys so deep
The air becomes thick, heavy and wet
No point going out as damp and cold you will get
The neighbourhood has disappeared, how long will this last?
Then finally the sun breaks through and gives it a blast
With the warmth of the sun, the wet wispy cloud will disappear
And the day will break out warm, sunny and clear.

Sayings

There's a couple of sayings I remember from my dad
One in particular when we had just done something bad
"My giddy Aunt" he used to say
Shaking his head, we knew trouble was on the way
He would comb his hands through his hair in total disbelief
And out came the belt, but the punishment was brief
The other one is, when I stop and think
With a look of amazement, he'd say "Strike me pink"
It was usually for something unexpected that had been done
And when this was uttered, we knew his affection we had won
There's probably many more, but just these two
Are the ones that I remember most out of the few

The Mail

The arrival of the mail was always an exciting thing
It only came twice a week and we never knew what it would bring
There were always newspapers and normally a bill or two
But even knowing this each time our excitement grew

Sometimes wrapped in brown paper a parcel there would be
It would be quickly ripped open its contents to see
A mysterious letter arrived with the post one morning
The light was still dim and the day was just dawning

The letter was placed on the table to be seen
It had many stamps on it from where it had been
From afar it had come, that was obvious to see
And it was addressed very official like to me

"Open it up dear" my mother had said
She was curious, as I was to see what it read
There were several pages of writing and something else too
But who it was from, I hadn't a clue

"Dear Sybil", it started and went on for a bit
And after a minute I said to Mum, "you had better sit"
My namesake in Canada had not long passed away
The letter informed me that I should travel there to stay

Her estate had been left to me on her death
I started to shake and took a deep breath
In total disbelief mum was shaking now too
We'd have to travel to Canada and see what to do

So, plans were made when we finally settled down
There were clothes we would need, we'd have to go into town
A few weeks later, we were on our way
To a small place called Calabogie, is where we would stay

It was a long trip to Ottawa, the lawyer to see
And he would take us where the house would be
Up in the mountains and at the edge of a lake
Was this beautiful house left by my namesake

Surrounded by trees and some snow on the ground
There were very few people in the area to be found
"stay here a while, I'll come back in a day or two
By then you'll have a decision on what you want to do

It was such a beautiful place with a small shop close by
With food and supplies we were able to buy
In winter heavy snow on the ground would cover
And the huge lake out the back would normally ice over

People would come to stay from miles around
It was apparently a very popular playground.
So, we sat and contemplated over a wine that night
And the decision we came to we felt was just right

We'd have to see, there was no way we could stay
As we had no idea if we'd ever come back this way
The lawyer came back just as he said he would
And after discussing our decision, he thought that was good.

Back to his office we went, papers to sign
Pleased in a way that this property wouldn't be mine
He'd transfer the funds as soon as it was sold
We were happy to head home and out of the cold

Thankyou my namesake Aunty, what a generous thing to do
The money would be a godsend and we'll for ever remember
you.

The Tooth Fairy

(Writers club assignment)

As a child I noticed at dinner one night
That one of my teeth did not feel quite right.
And although it wiggled, I could feel no pain,
I wondered when it would go and leave a gap again.

Would I have to tie a string around it like before,
Tie it to the handle and quickly slam the door?
But after a day and much to my relief,
It came out on its own and the discomfort was brief.

Under the pillow it went that night,
Would I hear the tooth fairy and wake up with a fright?
But no there was nothing to say,
That the tooth fairy had even been my way.

I searched under the pillow and alas there was no coin,
And the look on my face was one of forlorn.
The tooth fairy had certainly been, she'd left an envelope instead,
I quickly ripped it open and sat bolt up in bed.

The disappointment on my face disappeared in a flash,
As the envelope contained $50 in cash.
My excitement was clear, almost out of control,
I now had enough money to buy my first doll.

Thank you tooth fairy for knowing my dreams,
You must have plenty of money up there it seems.

Little Box of Ashes

Little box of ashes whose body did you hold
What were all the stories that will forever remain untold
Little box of ashes you may bring a tear to many an eye
As you died so suddenly, and we'll always wonder why
Little box of ashes that's really all that's left
Just another family left here grieving and bereft
Little box of ashes was there meaning in life for you
Did you leave your family a legacy, now that your life is
through
Little box of ashes you will soon be scattered free
Blown away in the wind, but that's not up to me
Little box of ashes, it's all come to that in the end
But eternity is now where the rest of your life will spend

The Starling Box

"We should, or rather you" I said to my husband one day
Build a starling box for their eggs to lay
He thought for a while and said he probably could
As in the shed there was still plenty of wood

I'll pop down the road when I can
There's a mate down there who'll have a plan
Then it was into the shed, the process to start
This starling box would be a work of art

The pieces were measured and measured again
Then a coat of paint to protect from the rain
And then another coat to slow down the wear and tear
Not that the starlings would notice or even care

Now it was ready to assemble and erect
It was looking great, everything was correct
Proudly erected on the fence the next day
We hoped the starlings would soon fly this way

A day or two it took them to find
Their beautiful nesting box to imprint on their minds
The early morning sun on their feathers would shine
As they sat on the perch and the nearby clothesline

Brilliant blues and greens would radiate in the sun
We could watch them for hours, it was such fun
Day after day they would fly in and out
And for bits of straw they were hunting about

With a beak full of straw they would land on the edge
They'd obviously been busy pecking in someone's hedge
Sometimes they would struggle to push the straw in
Then they'd flap their wings and kick their legs and finally
win

How proud they were sitting there up on high
Singing their songs to other birds passing by
When the eggs were laid we would be waiting to see
How many babies this year there would be
We knew they had hatched when the worms started to arrive
With the amount going in they were sure to survive
Then a cheep, cheep, cheep sound filled the air
The chicks were always hungry and the parents always near

In a couple of weeks, a little head would appear
It would have a look around and quickly disappear
The parents were so busy, not long would they stay
They'd take the poo out and then fly away

The mynahs would try and attach the small chicks
But we were onto them and knew all their tricks
We'd throw things at them, and the message was soon clear
That they were not welcome, anywhere near

Then one day we'd look out, no little face was there
The chicks had flown away with their parents somewhere
We decided that one box would certainly not do
So back to garage it was to make number two.

A Famous Saying

(Writers Group Challenge)

Are there times in life when you think this is it
What ever do you, you just don't seem to fit
You feel that your life is drifting away
And you can't go on, you can no longer stay

But the freedom is there it's etched in your mind
You have the power to leave evil behind
Maybe you have to fight hard to survive
But freedom is something to achieve and you must strive

"They may take our lives, but not our freedom", by
Braveheart was said
He had to inspire his soldiers so that death was not feared
There was many a man lost his life that day
And that call from Braveheart, was the last thing he would say

A Great Place To Go

It's well off the beaten track, I'd have to say
But the trip was worth it as you meander through country
roads on the way
This place is very special in so many ways
It brings back wonderful memories of my childhood days
It's a place out in the country called Waikaretu
It has significance to me, but probably not to you
It's on the coast in between Raglan and Port Waikato
And it's still a place that we all love to go.

See, I was raised on a farm out there in Waikaretu
With four brothers and a sister, there was always plenty to do
Sometimes over the hills to school, our horses we would ride
When the river was flooded, and the hills did subside
We'd venture to the coast as it was quite near
There was no one around for miles to bother us there

Dad would take us fishing, it was such a treat
Then we'd sit on the beach and fresh mussels we'd eat
There were 300 acres of native bush on the farm
We would explore for hours and not come to any harm
The air would be filled with the sweet scent of native trees

And we'd run through the grass which was up to our knees
Sometimes a wild pig would be roaming around
You could see where they'd been by the rooting on the ground

In the weekends there'd be picnics in a place by a stream
And all the local families would gather there it would seem
The children all swam in the fresh sparkling water
And we didn't want to go home when our folks said we oughta

Sports days at the school were always great fun
And in conjunction with other local schools, they were run
Our small country school, had 2 classrooms and 25 pupils or
so
And the school role would drop each year as off to boarding
school some would go

One of my brothers still lives out there today
The rest of the family have long since moved away
He has a farm with caves on and runs, with his wife, the Nikau
Café
And if you wanted to take some time out, there's
accommodation to stay

He takes many tourists each day through the caves
And has some funny stories to tell and a few close shaves
We still go out there often to reminisce and eat
As the pizza they make would be hard to beat
So, if you're looking for A GREAT PLACE TO GO,
You'll find a trip to Waikaretu enjoyable, I just know

Philippeans

Paul Wrote to the Philippians from his cell
He had so much thankfulness and love to tell
With years of discipline and intimate association with the master
He knew with Gods help they would avoid disaster

God, he said, cannot be contained or hoarded
Their spilling out of his love would only be rewarded
Learn to love appropriately and then your life should flourish
Use your head and test your feelings, and other people nourish

Live a lover's life, circumspect and exemplary
A life Jesus would be proud of and to him be complimentary
They cannot imprison the message, it's only the body there
Through faithful prayers and generous response, he will show that he does care

As long as we are alive, there is so much good work to be done
And not by just a chosen few, but by almost everyone
Stand united, singular in vision, your courage and unity will surely show through

Be a breath of fresh air in this squalled and polluted society
and teach the truth we should all pursue

The things once thought so important in life
Are meaningless compared to the privilege of knowing and
living in Christ
God will clear your blurred vision and put you back on track
Celebrate God all day, every day, revel in him and know he
has your back

Do not fret or worry, hand it up to God in prayer
He will help you though, he'll always be just there
You, Philippians, have been so gracious and helpful to all who
have been sent
And you'll surely be rewarded for the hours of prayers you've
spent

May you receive the amazing grace of the master deep within
your souls
And may you feel his strength within you as you take on
caring roles
So, when you sit quietly to read and contemplate his word
He may just open your heart and want to be heard

Opportunity

(A challenge from the writers' group)

Life itself is the greatest opportunity
It's the only chance you get, to be who you're meant to be
Are you open to seeing an opportunity when it comes along
It may be a really good one or it may be just so wrong

We need to have an open, enquiring mind
Check out all the possibilities and not go forward blind
If roadblocks come your way in what you're trying to do
This may not be the opportunity that is right for you

Sometimes an opportunity will arrive completely out of the blue
And will lead you on a journey to a place you never knew
These opportunities will challenge, excite and enable you to grow
And your success to the world you'll soon be able to show

Go boldly forth, it may not be all plain sailing
Don't ever be afraid of the outcome or even sometimes failing
Failing just means for you find another way
Keep your eyes on the end goal, let no-one lead you astray

The thrill of opportunities keeps your mind alive and well
Sometimes you may just have to step back and take a timely
spell
I urge you to keep an open eye for opportunities every day
But if you're sitting at home and not getting out, they'll never
come your way

The Mandarin Tree

We decided we'd like a mandarin tree, so off to the local garden shop we go
To see what they had in stock, there was very little on show
We did find a healthy specimen with some mandarins to pick
Took it home to plant and thought that should do the trick

The mandarins were free peel and very sweet
Maybe next year there'll be plenty more to eat
There was an old apple tree out the back taking up space
So we decided to dig it out and put the mandarin in its place

When it burst into bloom the following year
We waited in anticipation to see what it would bear
It was still a small tree so our expectations were not too high
But we'd still inspect the tree carefully each time we walked by

Imagine our surprise when the fruit just grew and grew
We had no idea what they were developing into
They certainly were a mandarin no longer
We had to tie up the branches to make it stronger

Many months went by and the fruit was ready to eat

It had turned into a naval orange tree, with fruit large and sweet

So little mandarin tree, what a triumph you have been

The lady at the garden centre could hardly believe what she had seen

Now we've brought another mandarin tree

Let's hope this one know what it is meant to be

Not There

(Writers group challenge)

A hunting trip we had planned for this day
We packed up all our gear, then went on our way
Up into the dense forests and the tree covered hills
We trudged for hours, wrapped warm against the winter chills

There was an old wooden hut set up among the trees
Which the owner said we could use whenever we please
Early the next morning just as the sun was breaking through
We donned our backpacks and headed for a hiding place we
knew

Here we'd stay a while as a view of a track was clear
And we knew this was often used by the wild deer
Nothing it seemed was passing here today
So, we moved on again and went another way

Walking along with my buddy I turned to speak
But he was nowhere to been seen, he'd fallen into a creek
Down a steep rocky slope, he'd stumbled and fallen
I could hear from down below a faint voice was calling

"Are you OK down there" I called out in alarm
Hoping he hadn't come to too much harm
"Everything is fine" he said "I'm not really hurt
When I finally reached him, he was covered in dirt

He brushed himself off and picked up his pack
Which in the fall had wrenched off his back
We'll look around in this area now that we are here
I think I saw some movement, it could possibly be deer

Before we moved on though, we stopped for a snack
Thank goodness we'd remembered to bring some food from
the shack
Rested a while we were ready to go
We crept through the bush, careful not to show

Up wind we stayed alert but calm
Then my buddy gently touched me on the arm
"up ahead" he said "I can hear a faint sound
Of footsteps moving across the rough ground

We quickly crouched down and in readiness we wait
I glance over and give the OK signal to my mate
We then catch a glimpse of a beast through the trees
We hold our breath, and stay still in the breeze

"He's yours" I whisper, and he takes him with one shot
He jumps up in excitement, it's the best he's ever got
We clamber over bracken to find this grand prey
And come to a standstill, as there in front of us it lay

My buddy was grinning from ear to ear
This was a story he would tell for many a year
Now the hard work was about to begin
As we cut up the beast and removed the skin

With its head on his shoulders hoisted high it was a wonderful
sight
There'd be free beer for all in the local pub tonight
Sweating and sore, dirty and tired
We finally made it out to our ride

Relieved of our burden our adrenalin still raced
There would be lots of questions to answer when our families
we faced
All the cuts and bruises would soon be bathed and cleaned
But not before on the local bar we had leaned
Getting into bed that night was heaven sent
But worth all the effort for the great day we had spent.

The Canadians

When we lived in Auckland, to the waterfront we'd go
Especially when the big cruise liners came in under tow
We always wondered where they had been
Where they were going and what had they seen

Ambling along the wharf one day a beautiful ship was there
An older couple approached us and asked if we were from
here
They wanted to know what sights and activities should be
seen
As they were staying a few nights and to look around they
were very keen

We're currently off work, would you like us to show around,
we said
Rather than getting a tour guide, it would be more fun instead
They thought this would be such a great idea
When they mentioned it to others, they were warned to take
care

You don't know these people, they said, you don't know what
they might do
There's a chance that they could take advantage of you
There was no fear from Gerri or John
As we hit it off when we first met and knew we'd get along

We picked them up early to take them out of town
Out into the countryside, to my brothers' farm to show them
around
He took them out on the back of the tractor, something they'd
never done
If they'd stayed in Auckland for the day, it wouldn't have
been nearly so much fun

We stopped at Pokeno for an ice cream on the way back
They couldn't believe the size of the ice cream stack
The next day we agreed to meet, a lunch they wanted to shout
As early the next morning they would be flying out

A deep and rewarding friendship was developed over many
years
They came over again and stayed with us, and departing there
was always tears
One year we decided that a white Christmas we'd like to try
And booked a holiday to Canada and into Ottawa we'd fly

After flight delays and a mighty snow storm
We finally arrived on a freezing cold dawn
It was 3am, snowing, dark and cold
It's not usually as bad as this, we were told

Finally, to their home not too far away
It would be a most delightful place to stay
On Christmas day Canada sure put on a show
The temperature had plummeted to 27 below

A feast was planned, the table was set
We'd meet lots of family, we'd not already met
But first there were presents, all piled up around a beautiful tree
We were given an early mulled wine, what a treat this was going to be

We all exchanged gifts, then it was upstairs to eat
I had decided for dessert to make a traditional Kiwi treat
The meat was a real triumph, everyone was more that well fed
And finally, when the guests went, we fell into our bed

It had been decided that in a day or two
They would take us up to Niagara and other sightseeing to do
The driveway was shovelled clear before we could head away
We'd booked into a hotel for a couple of days to stay

We stopped on the way to meet some more friends and a cup of tea
Awestruck with the snow and the countryside we would see
When we arrived at Niagara a bitter cold wind was blowing through
After braving the sight of the falls, then some shopping we would do

A beautiful tourist town called Little Niagara, was not far to
go
The shops were all in sale with their Christmas items on show
We had a good spend up on some unusual things we saw
Until we realised our cases would probably take no more

Then it was back to Ottawa, there were parties galore
And as big sales were on, we went shopping some more
When the day came that we'd have to depart
It was with many tears and a sadness of heart

Vancouver was the next stop and there we would stay
As our niece from Whistler would come down the next day
The snow was very heavy and we didn't know
If she would be able to make it on the roads she would go

She just made it through but had small window of time she
could stay
Until the roads would be impassible again up her way
We'd booked a short tour to have a look around
But many places were closed because of the snow on the
ground

They don't normally get such heavy snowstorms we were told
We were advised to stay indoors and out of the cold
Off to the airport we went the next day
We just sat on the tarmac, we couldn't get away

A blizzard had come through, they had the de-icing machines
out
There was nothing we could do, we couldn't even walk about
We sat there for hours waiting for a break in the cloud
And finally, were given the go-ahead and a take-off was
allowed
Eighteen hours it took before in Auckland we touched down
In the bright January sunshine, there was certainly no frown
We'd experienced our white Christmas, that's for sure
And we knew that we'd never want another one to endure

Give us the barbeques, beach and sunshine
We'll take that over another white Christmas any time.

The Out-House

Now Uncle Bill, he like to smoke
We used to call him a real good bloke
"You'll not smoke in here" Aunty said
"and you'll certainly not smoke while you're in bed

The out-house was in days of old
A long drop toilet at the end of the garden and out in the cold
At night to visit it was a perilous thing
Especially on the cold frosty nights during spring

Uncle Bill would leave smokes in the outhouse out back
In those days it was surrounded by a small wooden shack
Down the garden to the out- house he would carefully go
To have his smoke, so that no-one would know

With Uncle Bill's age his bladder was rather weak
So nearly every night, down to the out-house he would creep
He'd let out a sigh of delight as he lowered himself down
He could have a smoke now with no-one around

One night in particular he'd fallen asleep
And Aunty not noticing to the out-house did creep
She turned as she reached it to back in through the door
With her knickers half down, nearly reaching the floor

As she lowered herself down with relief to start to pee
Her husband asleep on the loo she did not see
He jumped up with a start and let out an almighty scream
It was a sight to behold and never again seen

Uncle Bill thought his luck was changing that night
But instead, it was Aunties wrath and a terrible fright
Needless to say Auntie always checked Uncle Bills bed
Before at night, she ventured out to the shed

The Nation

Our country has become so divided, it really breaks my heart
The crazy rules and mandates are tearing it apart
Our farmers are being punished and taxed to their last cent
And the resource management act, takes even more for their consent
The backbone of our country, the farmers have always been
They're struggling, tired and angry, with a bitterness rarely seen

Entrepreneurs we used to be known for, creative and alive
But now with all the regulations, it's a struggle to survive
Excessive spending with no accountability is rampant in our land
The money that we haven't got, slips out like shifting sand
Committees and consultants are engaged on projects at will
To see any results or progress, we are waiting on still

The roads are in a mess, big potholes and slips are not being repaired
If you're journeying through the country, you'd better be prepared
Make sure you have some food and water in the car with you

As you never know if the road may be closed and a detour
you'll have to do
It seems the people are angry like we've never seen before
Thank goodness there's an election soon as we cannot take
much more

Our vibrant exciting nation is in a recession, this we know
As the price increasing for our daily basics in the supermarket
show
The young and bright among us are going overseas
They've had enough of the struggles and want to create new
memories
I cannot believe how precious everyone has become
So many get upset now by everything and everyone

The health system or lack of it, I suppose
Is a total wreck, when that will be fixed heaven knows
Lives are put on hold while they wait for an appointment to
gain
And are taking more and more painkillers, just to relieve the
pain

We need to get our mojo back and take the lead again
Show the world we're back, and moved on from this financial
pain
Can someone please put an end to this malaise?
And steer our precious country out of this financial haze